Classic Tales

Level 3

The **Heron** and the **Hummingbird**

Activity Book and **Play**

 **Contents**

Name: _____

Class: _____   School: _____

OXFORD

UNIVERSITY PRESS

Activities

Before you read, can you write the words?

tree   river   fish   ~~heron~~   race   hummingbird   moon   flower

1

_____ heron _____

2

_____

3

_____

4

_____

5

_____

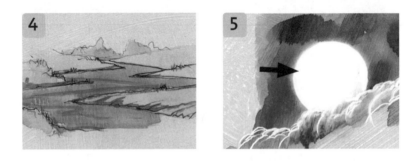

6

_____

7

_____

8

_____

1 Write the words.

| small different fish tall ~~good~~ |
| fast little lake strong big slow |

The heron and the hummingbird were _____good_____ friends,
but they were very _____. Heron was _____,
_____, and _____, and Hummingbird was
_____ and very _____. Heron and Hummingbird
loved to eat _____ from the _____. Heron
liked the _____ fish, and Hummingbird liked the
_____ fish.

2 Circle the mistake in each sentence. Then write the correct word.

1 The heron and the hummingbird lived (above) a lake.
   ____near____

2 One day Hummingbird said, 'There are not many fish in the
   lake for you and me.' _____

3 He said, 'Let's have a walk.' _____

4 He said, 'Let's swim for four days to the old tree near the river.'
   _____

5 'The loser of the race can have all the fish in the lake.'
   _____

6 Hummingbird was much slower than Heron. _____

7 Hummingbird knew he could win the race happily. _____

8 Heron was a kind bird, and he didn't like to say no to everyone.
   _____

9 So Heron said, 'That's a good word.' _____

1 Match, then complete the sentences with the past tense.

> fly   laugh   meet   do   say   stop   cry

> met   stopped   flew   cried   laughed   did   said

1 The next morning, Heron and Hummingbird _____met_____ at the lake.
2 'Good morning, my friend,' _____ Heron.
3 'You think you can fly faster than me, do you, Heron?' Hummingbird _____.
4 'Three, two, one ... Go!' Hummingbird _____.
5 The two birds _____ up above the lake.
6 Heron _____ not look down.
7 His long wings never _____ moving.

2 Find and write the words.

_____lake_____

_____

_____

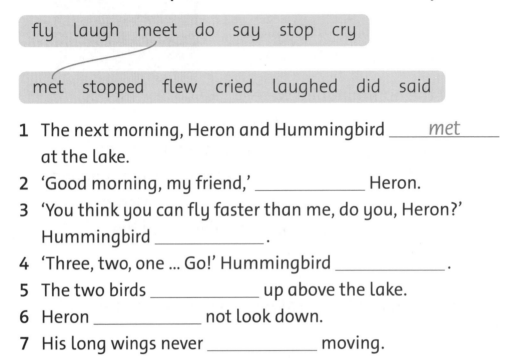

l	x	f	i	s	h
o	c	v	b	w	u
s	p	m	j	i	f
e	z	w	i	n	g
r	e	q	h	n	l
v	l	a	k	e	u
w	i	d	y	r	o

_____

_____

1 Answer the questions. Write *Yes* or *No*.

1 Did Hummingbird flutter? _____Yes._____

2 Did he fly slowly? _____

3 Did he fly fast? _____

4 Was he soon bored? _____

5 Were there some pretty flowers? _____

6 Did Hummingbird sometimes fly past them? _____

7 Did he drink from them? _____

8 Did Heron drink from the flowers? _____

9 Did Heron sometimes fly ahead of Hummingbird? _____

2 Circle the correct words. Then complete the sentences.

1 Hummingbird flew very fast, but he was _____soon_____ bored.

   once   nearly   (soon)

2 Every time he saw a pretty flower, he flew _____ and drank from it.

   down   around   away

3 Sometimes, when Hummingbird drank from the flowers, Heron flew _____ him.

   ahead of   through   above

4 When Hummingbird saw this, he flew quickly _____ Heron.

   under   after   into

5 And soon Hummingbird was _____ again.

   inside   behind   in front

6 'Why don't you fly _____ ?' Hummingbird called to Heron.

   happily   faster   better

→ Pages 8–9

1 Are the sentences correct? Circle *Yes* or *No*.

1 Heron laughed and called to Hummingbird.   Yes / (No)
2 When Hummingbird flew, he fluttered.   Yes / No
3 Heron flew slowly.   Yes / No
4 Hummingbird was strong.   Yes / No
5 Hummingbird never stopped.   Yes / No
6 Heron often stopped, because he was tired.   Yes / No
7 Hummingbird flew faster than Heron.   Yes / No
8 Heron flew up and down.   Yes / No
9 Heron slept all day.   Yes / No

2 Make sentences about the story.

1 Hummingbird looked at Heron behind him, and …

2 He thought, 'I'm going to …

3 All day the birds …

4 Heron flew slowly, but he was strong and he …

5 Hummingbird flew fast, but he …

a flew.

b win this race easily!'

c went up and down, up and down.

d laughed.

e never stopped.

→ Pages 10–11

1 Answer the questions.

1 What came at last? ___Evening.___

2 Why did Hummingbird stop for the night?

_____

3 Did Hummingbird want Heron to win the race? _____

4 Where did Hummingbird find a good place?

_____

5 Did Hummingbird think about Heron? _____

6 What did he think?

'I can soon _____

7 Soon what did Hummingbird do?

_____

8 Who flew all night? _____

9 What shone on the trees below?

_____

10 Did Heron look down or stop?

_____

2 Write the words and number the sentences 1–5.

asleep ~~tired~~ slow night tree

a ☐ Hummingbird thought, 'Heron is very _____.'

b ☐ Soon Hummingbird fell _____.

c ① Evening came, and Hummingbird was ___tired___.

d ☐ Heron didn't stop, and he flew all _____.

e ☐ Hummingbird found a good place in a _____.

1 Choose a, b, or c.

1 In the morning Hummingbird felt …
a ☐ bored   b ☐ sad   c ☑ good

2 He flew ahead of Heron and looked …
a ☐ away   b ☐ back   c ☐ out

3 Hummingbird laughed, 'Aren't you … , Heron?'
a ☐ tired   b ☐ pretty   c ☐ angry

4 Flap! Flap! Flap! The … heron flew all day.
a ☐ short   b ☐ big   c ☐ little

5 It was the … day of the race.
a ☐ first   b ☐ second   c ☐ third

6 Heron didn't stop or look …
a ☐ ahead   b ☐ out   c ☐ down

7 Hummingbird stopped and … the flowers.
a ☐ drank from   b ☐ played with   c ☐ slept in

2 Circle the mistake in each sentence. Then write the correct word.

1 Hummingbird slept (badly). _____well_____

2 In the morning Hummingbird flew quietly. _____

3 He soon caught Heron. _____

4 Heron said to him, 'Good morning, my brother.' _____

5 Hummingbird walked in front of Heron. _____

6 Hummingbird laughed, 'I'm in front of you sometimes!'

_____

7 Heron flew all day, and he always stopped. _____

8 Hummingbird drank from the dirty flowers. _____

9 Then he flew ahead into Heron once more. _____

1 Match, then complete the sentences with the past tense.

drink feel stop sleep think flutter fly call

thought flew called felt drank slept stopped fluttered

1 On the second night, Hummingbird _____slept_____ in a tree again.
2 On the third day, Hummingbird _____ in front of Heron again.
3 He _____ from the flowers.
4 Then he _____ near the big bird.
5 'Aren't you tired, Heron?' Hummingbird _____ .
6 On the third night, Hummingbird _____ in another tree.
7 'We're nearly at the river now,' he _____ .
8 Heron _____ a little wind on his wings, and he didn't stop.

2 What is Hummingbird thinking? Write the words.

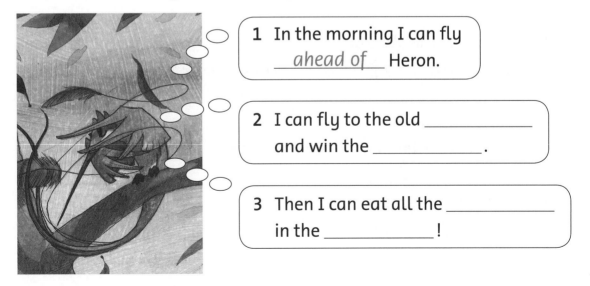

1 In the morning I can fly _____ahead of_____ Heron.

2 I can fly to the old _____ and win the _____ .

3 Then I can eat all the _____ in the _____ !

→ Pages 16–17

Circle the correct words. Then write sentences.

1 Who slept well again?

the fish ⟨Hummingbird⟩ Heron

Hummingbird slept well again.

2 Why couldn't Hummingbird fly well?

because it was very hot   because it was very cold

because it was very windy

Hummingbird couldn't _____

_____

3 What did he flutter faster and faster?

his feet   his head   his wings

_____

4 What pushed him back?

the tree   the wind   Heron

_____

5 Then what did Hummingbird see?

the lake   some pretty flowers   the old tree

_____

6 Where was the old tree?

near the river   by the lake   behind a house

_____

7 Where was Heron?

at the top of the tree   under the tree   by the tree

_____

8 So who was the winner?

Hummingbird   Heron   a boy

_____

1 Write the words.

1 tfsare ___*faster*___

2 wlef _____

3 inwd _____

4 ewninr _____

5 urhgny _____

6 akle _____

7 dakrn _____

8 erlosfw _____

9 lsitl _____

10 ravirde _____

11 trepyt _____

12 fshi _____

2 Put the words in the correct order.

1 am I faster much you than!
   I am much faster than you!

2 did get How here you?
   _____

3 I all night flew.
   _____

4 the drank from You flowers.
   _____

5 and stopped But I wind felt coming never the I.
   _____

6 old morning arrived I This tree the at.
   _____

7 ate Hummingbird again fish never.
   _____

8 the pretty He flew around flowers.
   _____

9 Now the had all in Heron fish lake the.
   _____

Play

Act the play.

Characters

Chorus

Heron

Hummingbird

→ Pages 2–3

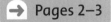

🍃 Scene 1 🍃

Chorus: The heron and the hummingbird lived near a big lake. Heron was tall, strong, and slow. Hummingbird was small and very fast. Heron and Hummingbird loved to eat fish from the lake. Heron liked the big fish, and Hummingbird liked the little fish.

🍃 Scene 2 🍃

Hummingbird: There are not enough fish in the lake for you and me. Let's have a race. Let's fly for four days to the old tree near the river. The winner of the race can have all the fish in the lake. The loser must never eat fish again.

Heron: That's a good idea.

🍃 *Scene 3* 🍃

Chorus: The next morning, Heron and Hummingbird met at the lake.

Heron: Good morning, my friend.

Hummingbird *(laughing)*: You think you can fly faster than me, do you, Heron? Remember, we are going to fly to the old tree near the river … Are you ready, Heron? Three, two, one … Go!

Chorus: The two birds flew up above the lake. *Flap! Flap! Flap!* Heron flew slowly, but he didn't look down. He just flew and flew.

Flutter! Flutter! Flutter! Hummingbird flew very fast, but he was soon bored. Every time he saw a pretty flower, he flew down and drank from it.

Sometimes, Heron flew ahead of Hummingbird. When Hummingbird saw this, he flew quickly after Heron, and soon he was in front again.

Hummingbird: Why don't you fly faster? Then you can drink from the flowers too! *(to himself)* I'm going to win this race easily!

Scene 4

Chorus: *Flap! Flap! Flap! Flutter! Flutter! Flutter!* All day the birds flew. Heron flew slowly, but he was strong and he never stopped. Hummingbird flew fast, but he went up and down, up and down.

Scene 5

Chorus: At last evening came. Hummingbird was tired, so he found a good place in a tree and stopped for the night.

Hummingbird: Heron is very slow. I can soon fly ahead of him in the morning.

Chorus: Soon Hummingbird fell asleep.

Scene 6

Chorus: Heron didn't stop. *Flap! Flap! Flap!* He flew all night. The big white moon shone on the trees below, but Heron didn't look down. He just flew and flew.

Scene 7

Chorus: Hummingbird slept well, and in the morning he felt good. He flew fast and he soon saw Heron.

Heron: Good morning, my friend.

Chorus: Hummingbird flew ahead and looked back.

Hummingbird (*laughing*): I'm in front of you again!

🌿 *Scene 8* 🌿

Chorus: *Flap! Flap! Flap!* All the second day, the big heron flew, and he never stopped or looked down. *Flutter! Flutter! Flutter!* The little hummingbird flew up and down. He stopped and drank from the pretty flowers, and then he flew ahead of Heron once more.

🌿 *Scene 9* 🌿

Chorus: On the second night, Hummingbird slept in a tree again, but Heron flew all night. And on the third day, Hummingbird flew in front of Heron again. He drank from the flowers and then fluttered near the big bird.

Hummingbird: Aren't you tired, Heron? Don't you want to stop?

🌿 *Scene 10* 🌿

Chorus: On the third night, Hummingbird stopped in another tree.

Hummingbird: We're nearly at the river now. In the morning I can win the race. Then I can eat all the fish in the lake!

Chorus: Heron was tired. But he felt a little wind on his wings, and he didn't stop. He just flew all night. *Flap! Flap! Flap!*

🍃 *Scene 11* 🍃

Chorus: The next morning Hummingbird felt good.

Hummingbird *(laughing)*: I'm going to win the race today!

Chorus: He flew after Heron. But it was very windy. Hummingbird fluttered his wings faster and faster, but the wind pushed him back.

Hummingbird: Where's Heron?

Chorus: He couldn't see Heron anywhere.

🍃 *Scene 12* 🍃

Chorus: Then Hummingbird saw the old tree. And at the top of the tree, he saw … Heron. Heron was the winner!

Hummingbird: I am much faster than you! How did you get here? How did you win?

Heron: I flew all night. You drank from the flowers and you slept. But I felt the wind coming and I never stopped. I'm tired and hungry, but I'm the winner.

🍃 *Scene 13* 🍃

Chorus: So after that, Hummingbird never ate fish again. Now Heron had all the fish in the lake. And this is why now, herons everywhere eat fish, and hummingbirds drink from flowers.

🍃 *The End* 🍃